Introduction to a Neurodiverse World

Avoidant/restrictive food intake disorder (ARFID)

Gareth Croot

Chapter 1: Introduction to ARFID

Avoidant/restrictive food intake disorder (ARFID) is a relatively newly recognised eating disorder that is characterised by an extreme picky eating or aversion to food. It was added to the fifth edition of the Diagnostic and Statistical Manual of Mental Disorders (DSM-5) in 2013, replacing the previous diagnosis of "feeding disorder of infancy or early childhood" (FED) (APA, 2013). ARFID has gained increasing recognition in the United Kingdom in recent years, with greater awareness of the condition among healthcare professionals and the general public.

ARFID is a distinct disorder from other eating disorders such as anorexia nervosa, bulimia nervosa, and binge eating disorder. Individuals with ARFID may avoid certain foods based on the food's sensory characteristics (such as texture, taste, or smell), fear of vomiting, or a general lack of interest in food. This can result in significant weight loss, nutritional deficiencies, and other medical complications. ARFID can affect individuals of all ages, but is most commonly diagnosed in children and adolescents.

The prevalence of ARFID is difficult to estimate due to the limited research on the disorder, but it is believed to be higher than previously thought. A study conducted by Nicholls and colleagues (2018) in the United Kingdom found that approximately 1.5% of children aged 7 to 9 years met the criteria for ARFID, which is higher than the estimated prevalence of anorexia nervosa in the same age group. It is possible that many individuals with ARFID go undiagnosed or misdiagnosed, particularly if they do not meet the strict criteria for other eating disorders.

The diagnosis of ARFID requires a thorough assessment by a healthcare professional, typically a psychiatrist, psychologist or dietitian. Diagnosis involves the exclusion of other medical and psychiatric conditions, such as gastrointestinal disorders or autism spectrum disorder, that could account for the individual's symptoms. The individual must also demonstrate one or more of the following behaviours: avoidance or restriction of food intake, an inability to meet nutritional requirements, and significant interference with daily functioning or socialisation. In addition, the individual's symptoms must not be better explained by another psychiatric disorder or due to a cultural practice or lack of available food.

ARFID can have significant impacts on both physical and mental health. As individuals with ARFID avoid or restrict certain foods, they can experience nutritional deficiencies that can lead to a range of medical complications such as growth impairment, anaemia, and weakened immune system. ARFID can also cause significant psychological distress, including anxiety, depression, and social isolation. For children and adolescents, ARFID can impact development and growth. For adults, ARFID can impact their ability to work, socialise, and maintain relationships.

Treatment for ARFID typically involves a multidisciplinary approach, with input from mental health professionals, dietitians, and primary care physicians. The treatment approach will depend on the individual's symptoms and severity of their condition. Cognitive behavioural therapy (CBT) is one of the most commonly used therapies to treat ARFID. CBT focuses on changing the individual's thoughts and behaviours related to food, and involves exposure to new or avoided foods in a gradual and structured way. Family-based therapy (FBT) can also be effective for children and adolescents with ARFID, where the family plays an active role in supporting the individual to increase their food intake.

In addition to therapy, nutritional support such as tube feeding or nutritional supplements may be required to address any nutritional deficiencies. Medication can also be used to treat ARFID, such as medications to address anxiety or depression. Treatment for ARFID can be a long and difficult process, but with proper care and support, individuals with ARFID can make significant progress towards recovery.

The United Kingdom has seen some progress in the recognition and treatment of ARFID in recent years. The National Institute for Health and Care Excellence (NICE) released guidelines for the treatment of eating disorders in 2017, which included recommendations for the assessment and management of ARFID (NICE, 2017). These guidelines highlighted the importance of early identification and intervention, as well as the need for a multidisciplinary approach to treatment.

Despite these developments, there is still a need for greater awareness and understanding of ARFID in the United Kingdom. Many healthcare professionals may not be familiar with the disorder or may mistake it for other conditions, such as picky eating or disordered eating. There is also a lack of specialised treatment centres for individuals with ARFID, particularly outside of major cities.

Furthermore, there are specific challenges to addressing ARFID in the United Kingdom. The country's cultural and culinary diversity can make it difficult to provide appropriate nutritional care for individuals with ARFID. In addition, the UK's National Health Service (NHS) is under significant strain and resources for mental health services are limited, which can make it difficult for individuals with ARFID to access the care they need.

Chapter 2: History of ARFID

Avoidant/Restrictive Food Intake Disorder (ARFID) is a relatively new diagnostic category, officially recognized in the fifth edition of the Diagnostic and Statistical Manual of Mental Disorders (DSM-5) published in 2013. However, the concept of ARFID can be traced back to earlier research and classifications.

In the UK, ARFID was previously known as Selective Eating Disorder (SED), a term coined in the 1990s by Dr. Jennifer J. Thomas, a clinical psychologist and expert in eating disorders. SED was initially proposed as a separate diagnostic category for individuals who exhibited selective food intake without the fear of weight gain or body image disturbance associated with other eating disorders.

However, the term SED was not widely adopted in the UK or other parts of the world. Instead, the condition was often referred to as "picky eating" or "food phobia," which did not accurately reflect the complexity or severity of the disorder. As a result, many individuals with ARFID were overlooked or misdiagnosed, and did not receive appropriate treatment.

In 2013, the American Psychiatric Association (APA) introduced ARFID as a new diagnostic category in the DSM-5. ARFID replaced the term "feeding disorder of infancy or early childhood," which was often used to describe individuals who exhibited selective or restricted eating patterns beyond early childhood.

The introduction of ARFID as a distinct diagnostic category was a significant step forward in recognizing the unique features and complexities of the disorder. The diagnosis requires persistent and extreme avoidance or restriction of food intake, resulting in weight loss or nutritional deficiency, without the fear of weight gain or body image disturbance that characterizes other eating disorders.

Since the introduction of ARFID in the DSM-5, there has been increasing awareness and recognition of the disorder in the UK and worldwide. In 2018, the National Institute for Health and Care Excellence (NICE) published guidelines on the recognition and management of eating disorders, which included recommendations for the assessment and treatment of ARFID.

However, despite these advancements, there is still a lack of understanding and awareness of ARFID among healthcare professionals and the general public. Many individuals with ARFID continue to be misdiagnosed or undertreated, resulting in prolonged suffering and negative impacts on physical and mental health.

There are several factors that may contribute to the under-recognition and under-treatment of ARFID in the UK. First, the diagnostic criteria for ARFID are still relatively new and unfamiliar to many healthcare professionals. Second, the presentation of ARFID can be diverse and complex, and may overlap with other eating disorders or mental health conditions. Third, there is a lack of specialist services and resources for the assessment and treatment of ARFID in many parts of the UK, particularly outside of major cities.

To address these challenges, it is essential to increase awareness and education around ARFID among healthcare professionals and the general public. This can include providing training and resources on the recognition and management of ARFID, as well as raising public awareness through campaigns and media coverage.

In addition, it is important to develop specialized services and resources for the assessment and treatment of ARFID, particularly in areas where access to specialist services may be limited. This can include multidisciplinary teams with expertise in eating disorders, as well as resources for families and caregivers.

Furthermore, research into the causes and treatment of ARFID is essential to advance our understanding of the disorder and improve outcomes for individuals with ARFID. This can include studies into the genetic and environmental factors that may contribute to the development of ARFID, as well as the efficacy of different treatment approaches.

Chapter 3: Causes of ARFID

In recent years, there has been growing interest in understanding the causes of Avoidant/Restrictive Food Intake Disorder (ARFID) in the UK. ARFID is a relatively new diagnosis, and there is still much that is unknown about its underlying causes. However, there are several potential factors that have been identified as contributing to the development of ARFID.

Genetic and Neurobiological Factors

Research has suggested that there may be a genetic component to ARFID. A study conducted by the University of Chicago found that individuals with ARFID were more likely to have a family history of eating disorders, suggesting that there may be a genetic predisposition to developing the condition. Other research has suggested that there may be neurobiological factors at play. For example, one study found that individuals with ARFID had differences in brain function compared to individuals without the disorder. Specifically, they showed less activation in the areas of the brain associated with reward processing and food motivation. These findings suggest that there may be a biological basis for the development of ARFID.

Environmental Factors

There are also several environmental factors that have been linked to the development of ARFID. One such factor is trauma. Research has suggested that individuals who have experienced trauma, particularly in childhood, may be at a higher risk of developing ARFID. This may be due to the fact that trauma can lead to a heightened sense of anxiety, which can manifest as avoidance of certain foods. Other environmental factors that may contribute to the development of ARFID include parental feeding practices, cultural and societal attitudes towards food, and exposure to stressful or traumatic events.

Psychological Factors

Psychological factors have also been identified as potential contributors to the development of ARFID. For example, individuals with ARFID may have anxiety or phobias related to food, which can lead to avoidance or restriction of certain foods. Additionally, individuals with ARFID may have a history of anxiety or obsessive-compulsive disorder (OCD), which can also contribute to the development of the disorder.

ARFID and Autism Spectrum Disorder (ASD)

There is a significant overlap between ARFID and Autism Spectrum Disorder (ASD), and many individuals with ARFID also have a diagnosis of ASD. Research has suggested that there may be shared underlying neurobiological factors between the two conditions. For example, both ARFID and ASD have been linked to differences in brain function, particularly in the areas of the brain associated with social communication and emotional regulation. Additionally, both conditions have been associated with sensory processing difficulties, which may contribute to the avoidance of certain foods.

Diagnosing the Underlying Causes of ARFID

Given the complexity of the underlying causes of ARFID, it can be challenging to accurately diagnose the disorder. However, a thorough assessment of the individual's medical history, nutritional status, and psychological functioning can help to identify potential contributing factors. This may involve conducting medical tests to rule out any underlying medical conditions, as well as psychological assessments to evaluate for anxiety, depression, OCD, or other psychological factors.

Treatment for ARFID

The treatment for ARFID in the UK is typically multi-disciplinary, involving a team of healthcare professionals, including a doctor, dietitian, and therapist. The specific treatment approach will depend on the individual's needs and underlying causes of the disorder.

Cognitive Behavioural Therapy (CBT) is a commonly used therapy for ARFID in the UK. This approach focuses on helping individuals to change their thoughts and behaviours related to food, and to gradually increase their comfort with new foods. Exposure therapy is often used in conjunction with CBT, where individuals are gradually exposed to new foods in a controlled setting.

Chapter 4: Diagnosis and Assessment of ARFID

In the United Kingdom, ARFID is a relatively new diagnosis that was introduced in the fifth edition of the Diagnostic and Statistical Manual of Mental Disorders (DSM-5) in 2013. Since its introduction, there has been a growing awareness of the condition among healthcare professionals in the UK.

Diagnosis of ARFID involves a comprehensive assessment that considers the individual's symptoms, medical history, and nutritional status. The assessment process typically involves a multidisciplinary team, including a physician, a psychologist, and a dietitian.

One of the key diagnostic criteria for ARFID is a restricted or highly selective eating pattern that leads to inadequate nutrient intake and/or weight loss or failure to achieve expected weight gain or growth. The individual may refuse to eat certain foods based on their sensory characteristics, such as texture, smell, or taste, or due to a fear of choking or vomiting. They may also have a lack of interest in eating or may experience significant anxiety around mealtimes.

Another important criterion for ARFID is that the individual's eating behaviors must not be better explained by another medical or psychiatric condition, such as anorexia nervosa, bulimia nervosa, or a food allergy or intolerance. This can be challenging, as individuals with ARFID often have co-occurring conditions that may complicate diagnosis and treatment.

The assessment process for ARFID typically involves a thorough medical evaluation, including a physical examination and blood tests to assess nutritional status. A psychological evaluation may also be conducted to assess for co-occurring mental health conditions, such as anxiety or depression, and to explore the individual's attitudes and beliefs around food and eating.

A key component of the assessment process is the evaluation of the individual's nutritional status. This may involve measuring their height, weight, and body mass index (BMI), as well as assessing their intake of key nutrients such as protein, vitamins, and minerals. A registered dietitian can play a crucial role in this process, providing guidance on appropriate food choices and nutritional supplements to help address any deficiencies.

Another important aspect of the assessment process is the evaluation of the individual's feeding environment. This includes an assessment of the family's attitudes and beliefs around food and eating, as well as any potential environmental factors that may be contributing to the individual's restricted eating pattern, such as food insecurity or poverty.

In the UK, there is growing recognition of the need for specialist services to diagnose and treat ARFID. While there are some general services available, there are currently no dedicated services for the treatment of ARFID in the NHS. As a result, many individuals with ARFID may not receive the specialist care they need.

There are, however, some private services available that specialize in the treatment of ARFID, including outpatient clinics and day programs. These services typically provide a multidisciplinary approach to treatment, including psychotherapy, nutritional support, and exposure therapy to gradually introduce new foods.

It is also important to note that in the UK, there is still some stigma attached to the diagnosis of ARFID. Many individuals with the condition may feel misunderstood or dismissed by healthcare professionals, and may struggle to access appropriate treatment and support. As such, there is a need for greater awareness and understanding of ARFID among healthcare professionals and the wider public.

Chapter 5: Co-occurring Conditions with ARFID

ARFID often co-occurs with other mental health conditions, including anxiety, depression, OCD, and autism spectrum disorder. In the UK, research has shown that up to 75% of individuals with ARFID have at least one additional psychiatric diagnosis. Understanding these co-occurring conditions is important for effective treatment and management of ARFID.

Anxiety is one of the most common co-occurring conditions with ARFID. In the UK, anxiety disorders are the most prevalent mental health condition, affecting approximately 1 in 6 adults. For individuals with ARFID, anxiety can manifest in a variety of ways, including fear of choking, fear of vomiting, and fear of new foods. This can make it difficult for individuals with ARFID to try new foods or participate in social situations involving food. Anxiety can also contribute to the development and maintenance of ARFID, as individuals may avoid certain foods or food groups due to anxiety-related fears.

Depression is another common co-occurring condition with ARFID. In the UK, depression is estimated to affect around 1 in 5 adults. For individuals with ARFID, depression can be a result of the social isolation and shame that often accompany the condition. Individuals with ARFID may feel embarrassed or ashamed of their restricted diet, which can lead to social withdrawal and depression. In some cases, depression may also contribute to the development of ARFID, as individuals may lose interest in food or experience changes in appetite as a result of their depression.

OCD is also commonly co-occurring with ARFID. In the UK, OCD affects approximately 1 in 50 adults. For individuals with ARFID, OCD can manifest in a variety of ways, including obsessive thoughts about food safety and contamination, and compulsive rituals related to food preparation or consumption. Individuals with ARFID may have rigid rules about food, such as only eating food of a certain color or texture, and may become distressed if these rules are not followed. These rigid rules and compulsive behaviors can make it difficult for individuals with ARFID to try new foods or engage in flexible eating patterns.

Autism spectrum disorder (ASD) is also frequently co-occurring with ARFID. In the UK, ASD affects around 1 in 100 adults. Individuals with ASD may have sensory sensitivities or aversions that make it difficult for them to tolerate certain foods or textures. They may also struggle with the social aspects of eating, such as table manners and etiquette. For individuals with ASD and ARFID, the combination of sensory sensitivities and rigid rules around food can make it particularly challenging to expand their food choices and engage in flexible eating patterns.

The co-occurrence of these conditions with ARFID can complicate treatment and management. In the UK, a multidisciplinary approach is often used to address the complex needs of individuals with ARFID and co-occurring conditions. This may involve collaboration between mental health professionals, dietitians, and other healthcare providers. Treatment may include a combination of psychotherapy, medication, and nutritional support.

Cognitive behavioral therapy (CBT) is a commonly used psychotherapy for individuals with ARFID and co-occurring conditions. In the UK, CBT is often provided by mental health professionals such as clinical psychologists or cognitive behavioral therapists. CBT for ARFID may focus on identifying and challenging negative thoughts and beliefs around food, as well as developing skills for coping with anxiety and other co-occurring conditions.

Medication may also be used to treat co-occurring conditions in individuals with ARFID. In the UK, medication for anxiety and depression is often prescribed by a psychiatrist or general practitioner. Selective serotonin reuptake inhibitors (SSRIs) are a type of medication commonly used to treat anxiety and depression. In some cases, medication may also be used to treat symptoms of OCD or ASD that co-occur with ARFID.

Nutritional support is another important component of treatment for individuals with ARFID and co-occurring conditions. In the UK, dietitians are often involved in the treatment of ARFID. They can provide guidance on how to meet nutritional needs despite a restricted diet, as well as how to expand food choices in a gradual and supportive manner. Nutritional support may also involve the use of nutritional supplements or meal replacement shakes to ensure that individuals are meeting their nutrient needs.

In addition to these formal treatment approaches, there are also a number of self-help strategies that individuals with ARFID and co-occurring conditions can use to manage their symptoms. These may include relaxation techniques such as deep breathing or meditation to manage anxiety, and structured meal planning to provide structure and predictability around mealtimes.

It is also important to seek support from friends and family members, as well as peer support groups. In the UK, there are a number of organizations that provide support and resources for individuals with ARFID and their loved ones, such as the National Centre for Eating Disorders and Beat.

Chapter 6: Impact of ARFID on Physical Health

ARFID can have a significant impact on physical health, particularly if left untreated. As the name suggests, Avoidant/Restrictive Food Intake Disorder is characterised by a persistent lack of interest in food or an aversion to certain foods, leading to inadequate nutrient intake and subsequent health complications. In this chapter, we will discuss the potential physical health consequences of ARFID and the impact it can have on the body.

Malnutrition

One of the most significant physical consequences of ARFID is malnutrition. Malnutrition can occur when the body does not receive enough nutrients, either due to insufficient intake or an inability to absorb nutrients properly. Inadequate nutrient intake can lead to a range of deficiencies, including protein, vitamin, and mineral deficiencies, which can have a cascading effect on the body's functions.

Protein deficiencies, for example, can lead to muscle weakness, fatigue, and reduced immune function. Iron deficiency can lead to anaemia, which can cause fatigue, shortness of breath, and cognitive impairments. Similarly, vitamin D deficiency can lead to rickets in children and osteomalacia in adults, causing bone pain, muscle weakness, and fractures. Nutrient deficiencies can also affect the brain, causing cognitive impairments and affecting mood.

Growth and Development

ARFID can also affect growth and development, particularly in children and adolescents. Inadequate nutrient intake can lead to stunted growth and delayed development. In extreme cases, it can even lead to failure to thrive, a condition characterised by significant weight loss and developmental delays.

Inadequate nutrient intake can also affect bone development, particularly if calcium and vitamin D intake is insufficient. This can increase the risk of bone fractures, particularly in children and adolescents who are still growing.

Gastrointestinal Complications

ARFID can also lead to a range of gastrointestinal complications, particularly if the individual restricts certain food groups or has an aversion to certain textures. Avoidance of fibre-rich foods, for example, can lead to constipation, while excessive consumption of processed foods can lead to diarrhoea and other digestive issues.

Additionally, restrictive eating patterns can lead to delayed gastric emptying, where food takes longer to pass through the digestive system. This can cause bloating, nausea, and abdominal pain. Prolonged restrictive eating patterns can also cause the stomach to shrink, making it difficult for the individual to consume normal-sized meals.

Dental Complications

ARFID can also lead to dental complications, particularly if the individual restricts certain food groups or has a preference for soft, processed foods. Avoidance of calcium-rich foods, for example, can lead to tooth decay and cavities, while excessive consumption of sugary foods can also cause dental problems.

Additionally, individuals with ARFID may be more prone to oral health problems if they avoid brushing their teeth or using mouthwash due to a dislike of certain tastes or textures. This can lead to a build-up of bacteria and plaque, increasing the risk of dental problems.

Impact on Mental Health

The physical consequences of ARFID can also have a significant impact on mental health. Nutrient deficiencies, for example, can cause cognitive impairments and affect mood, leading to anxiety and depression. Similarly, physical symptoms such as fatigue, muscle weakness, and abdominal pain can also impact mental health, affecting quality of life and leading to feelings of frustration and hopelessness.

The impact on mental health can be particularly significant for children and adolescents, who may struggle to understand and communicate their feelings. As a result, it is important for healthcare professionals to consider the potential impact on mental health when treating ARFID and to provide appropriate support and resources.

Treatment and Prevention

Treating ARFID early is crucial to prevent the physical and mental health consequences outlined above. Treatment may involve working with a healthcare professional, such as a dietitian or therapist, to gradually increase the individual's exposure to new foods and expand their food repertoire. In some cases, supplements may also be prescribed to address nutrient deficiencies.

Prevention is also important, particularly in children and adolescents. Encouraging a positive relationship with food from a young age, including exposure to a variety of foods and regular mealtimes, can help to prevent the development of ARFID. Additionally, it is important to address any aversions or food-related anxiety early, to prevent them from developing into a more severe disorder.

Chapter 7: Impact of ARFID on Mental Health

Avoidant Restrictive Food Intake Disorder (ARFID) can have a significant impact on mental health, both in the short and long-term. In the UK, as in other countries, ARFID is often misunderstood or misdiagnosed, which can compound the negative effects on mental health. This chapter will explore the ways in which ARFID can impact mental health in the UK and what resources are available for individuals seeking help.

The Impact of ARFID on Mental Health

ARFID can impact mental health in a number of ways. Firstly, the anxiety and fear associated with trying new foods can lead to social isolation and feelings of shame or embarrassment. Individuals with ARFID may avoid social situations that involve food, which can lead to feelings of loneliness and depression.

Furthermore, the restricted food intake associated with ARFID can lead to malnutrition and a host of physical health problems. The combination of physical and mental health issues can be overwhelming, leading to increased anxiety and depression.

In the long-term, ARFID can lead to a distorted relationship with food, which can have negative effects on mental health. The fear of certain foods can become deeply ingrained, leading to difficulty in establishing a healthy relationship with food. Individuals with ARFID may experience feelings of guilt or shame when they eat certain foods, even if they are not harmful or unhealthy.

The Impact of Misunderstanding and Misdiagnosis

ARFID is still a relatively new diagnosis, and many healthcare professionals in the UK may not be familiar with the condition. This can lead to misdiagnosis or a lack of diagnosis, which can exacerbate the negative effects on mental health.

Furthermore, many individuals with ARFID may not recognise that they have a problem or may be ashamed to seek help. The stigma surrounding eating disorders in the UK can make it difficult for individuals to open up about their struggles with food, which can delay diagnosis and treatment.

The lack of understanding and resources for ARFID in the UK can also make it difficult for individuals to access appropriate treatment. Many healthcare professionals may not be familiar with the latest research or treatment methods for ARFID, which can lead to suboptimal care.

Resources for Help

Despite the challenges of accessing appropriate care for ARFID in the UK, there are resources available for individuals seeking help. The National Health Service (NHS) provides mental health services for individuals struggling with eating disorders, including ARFID. These services may include counselling, cognitive behavioural therapy (CBT), and nutritional support.

There are also a number of charities and organisations in the UK that provide support and resources for individuals with ARFID and their families. These include the National Eating Disorders Association, Beat, and the Eating Disorders Association.

Additionally, support groups can be a valuable resource for individuals with ARFID. These groups provide a safe space for individuals to share their experiences and connect with others who are struggling with similar issues. The National Centre for Eating Disorders in the UK provides a list of support groups and resources for individuals with ARFID.

Conclusion

ARFID can have a significant impact on mental health in the UK. The anxiety and fear associated with trying new foods, combined with the physical health consequences of restricted food intake, can lead to depression, anxiety, and social isolation. The lack of understanding and resources for ARFID in the UK can exacerbate these negative effects, making it difficult for individuals to access appropriate care.

Despite these challenges, there are resources available for individuals seeking help. The NHS, charities, organisations, and support groups can provide valuable support and resources for individuals with ARFID and their families. By increasing awareness and understanding of ARFID in the UK, we can work towards improving diagnosis and treatment options, as well as reducing the stigma surrounding eating disorders.

It is important for healthcare professionals in the UK to receive adequate education and training on ARFID to ensure that individuals receive the appropriate care they need. Additionally, increased awareness and understanding of ARFID can help individuals feel more comfortable seeking help and reduce the shame and stigma surrounding the condition.

Chapter 8: ARFID in Children and Adolescents (UK Perspective)

Avoidant/Restrictive Food Intake Disorder (ARFID) is a relatively new diagnosis, having been officially recognised in the Diagnostic and Statistical Manual of Mental Disorders, Fifth Edition (DSM-5) in 2013. It is a disorder that can occur in children and adolescents, and can have significant implications for their health and development. In this chapter, we will explore ARFID from a UK perspective, including its prevalence, diagnosis, and treatment options.

Prevalence

The exact prevalence of ARFID in the UK is unknown, as there have been no large-scale epidemiological studies conducted to date. However, it is believed to be relatively common, with estimates suggesting that it may affect up to 5% of children and adolescents.

ARFID is often underdiagnosed, due to a lack of awareness and understanding among healthcare professionals. Many children and adolescents with ARFID may be misdiagnosed with other conditions, such as picky eating or anorexia nervosa, which can delay appropriate treatment and support.

Diagnosis

The diagnosis of ARFID requires a thorough assessment by a healthcare professional, such as a paediatrician, child psychiatrist, or clinical psychologist. The assessment should include a detailed medical and developmental history, a physical examination, and a comprehensive evaluation of the child or adolescent's eating behaviours and attitudes.

The DSM-5 diagnostic criteria for ARFID include:

- Persistent failure to meet appropriate nutritional and/or energy needs, leading to significant weight loss, nutritional deficiency, dependence on oral nutritional supplements, or other medical complications.
- The eating disturbance is not attributable to a lack of available food or cultural or religious practices.
- The eating disturbance is not better explained by anorexia nervosa or bulimia nervosa.
- The eating disturbance does not occur exclusively during the course of another mental disorder (e.g., autism spectrum disorder, intellectual disability, etc.).
- The eating disturbance is not due to a general medical condition or medication.

It is important to note that the diagnostic criteria for ARFID may differ slightly in the UK, as healthcare professionals may use different classification systems or guidelines. However, the overall aim of the assessment is to identify the underlying causes of the child or adolescent's eating difficulties, and to develop a tailored treatment plan.

Treatment

The treatment of ARFID in children and adolescents typically involves a multidisciplinary approach, with input from a range of healthcare professionals, such as paediatricians, child psychiatrists, clinical psychologists, dietitians, and occupational therapists.

The choice of treatment will depend on the individual needs of the child or adolescent, and may include one or more of the following interventions:

Behavioural interventions: Behavioural interventions, such as exposure therapy or systematic desensitisation, aim to increase the child or adolescent's exposure to new or previously avoided foods in a controlled and supportive environment. This can help to reduce anxiety and increase confidence around food.

Nutritional support: Nutritional support may be necessary in cases where the child or adolescent is severely malnourished or has significant medical complications. This may involve the use of oral nutritional supplements, nasogastric or gastrostomy feeding, or other forms of enteral or parenteral nutrition.

Medication: Medication may be used in some cases to address specific symptoms or comorbidities associated with ARFID, such as anxiety or depression. However, medication should be used with caution in children and adolescents, and should always be prescribed by a qualified healthcare professional.

Family-based interventions: Family-based interventions, such as the Maudsley Approach or Family Therapy, involve working with the whole family to address the child or communication, reducing conflict around meal times, and encouraging the child or adolescent to take an active role in their own recovery.

Occupational therapy: Occupational therapy can be useful for children and adolescents with ARFID who have sensory issues or difficulties with fine motor skills, which can affect their ability to eat. Occupational therapists can provide individualised interventions to help improve these skills and support the child or adolescent's overall development.

It is important to note that treatment for ARFID can be a long and challenging process, and may require ongoing support and monitoring. It is also important to involve the child or adolescent in the decision-making process and to respect their preferences and needs.

In the UK, there are a number of specialist services and resources available for children and adolescents with ARFID and their families. These include:

The NHS Eating Disorders Service: The NHS Eating Disorders Service provides specialist support for children and adolescents with ARFID, as well as other eating disorders. The service may include outpatient, day-patient or inpatient treatment, depending on the severity of the condition.

The National Centre for Eating Disorders: The National Centre for Eating Disorders provides information and resources on eating disorders, including ARFID. They offer online courses and workshops for healthcare professionals and individuals affected by ARFID.

Beat: Beat is a UK-based charity that provides support and information for people with eating disorders, as well as their families and friends. They offer a helpline, online support groups, and resources on a range of eating disorders, including ARFID.

Avoidant/Restrictive Food Intake Disorder (ARFID) is a relatively newly recognised eating disorder that has only recently gained recognition in the UK. It is characterised by an aversion to certain foods or types of food, as well as a lack of interest in eating and/or difficulty eating certain foods. In this chapter, we will discuss the unique challenges faced by individuals with ARFID in the UK and the various treatment options available.

Prevalence of ARFID in the UK

ARFID is relatively new to the UK, and research into the prevalence of the disorder is limited. However, a study conducted in the UK found that 1.5% of children aged 7-9 met the diagnostic criteria for ARFID (Norris et al., 2018). It is likely that the prevalence of ARFID in the UK is similar to that of other countries, but more research is needed to determine this.

Challenges of ARFID in the UK

One of the major challenges of ARFID in the UK is a lack of recognition and awareness of the disorder. Many healthcare professionals in the UK are still unfamiliar with ARFID, which can lead to delayed or misdiagnosis. This lack of awareness can also contribute to a lack of appropriate treatment options.

Additionally, the UK's healthcare system presents its own unique challenges. The National Health Service (NHS) has limited resources and waiting lists for eating disorder treatment can be long. This can lead to delays in treatment, which can be detrimental to individuals with ARFID who may require urgent intervention.

Treatment Options for ARFID

In the UK, treatment for ARFID typically involves a multidisciplinary approach, with a team of healthcare professionals working together to address the various aspects of the disorder. Treatment may include psychological therapy, nutritional support, and medical intervention if necessary.

Psychological Therapy

Cognitive Behavioural Therapy (CBT) is the most commonly used psychological therapy for ARFID in the UK. CBT focuses on challenging and changing negative thoughts and behaviours related to food and eating. This can include exposure therapy, where the individual is gradually exposed to feared or avoided foods in a controlled environment.

Family-based Treatment (FBT) is another psychological therapy that is commonly used for children and adolescents with ARFID. FBT involves the family in the treatment process and focuses on gradually reintroducing a wider range of foods into the child's diet.

Nutritional Support

Nutritional support is an important aspect of treatment for ARFID, particularly if the individual is malnourished or at risk of malnourishment. This may involve the use of supplements or tube feeding, depending on the individual's needs.

Medical Intervention

In some cases, medical intervention may be necessary for individuals with ARFID. This may include hospitalisation for refeeding and stabilisation of physical health, or the use of medication to address co-occurring conditions such as anxiety or depression.

Challenges of accessing treatment

As previously mentioned, the UK's healthcare system presents unique challenges when it comes to accessing treatment for ARFID. The NHS has limited resources and waiting lists for eating disorder treatment can be long. This can result in delayed or inadequate treatment, which can be detrimental to individuals with ARFID.

Additionally, the COVID-19 pandemic has had a significant impact on the availability of eating disorder treatment in the UK. Many services have been disrupted or reduced, and individuals with ARFID may face even longer waiting times for treatment.

Chapter 10: Treatment for ARFID

ARFID can be a challenging disorder to treat, and effective treatment requires a collaborative effort between healthcare professionals, individuals with ARFID, and their families and caregivers. There are several treatment options available for ARFID, including psychotherapy, medication, and nutritional support. In this chapter, we will explore these treatment options from a UK bias.

Psychotherapy

Psychotherapy is a common treatment option for ARFID, and several types of psychotherapy have been shown to be effective in treating the disorder. Cognitive behavioral therapy (CBT) is one such therapy that has been used to treat ARFID.

CBT is a structured therapy that helps individuals change their thoughts and behaviours related to food. In ARFID, CBT can help individuals identify and challenge negative thoughts and fears about food and eating, and develop more positive and adaptive attitudes and behaviours.

In the UK, CBT is often provided by mental health professionals such as clinical psychologists or cognitive behavioral therapists. Typically, individuals with ARFID will attend weekly sessions with their therapist over a period of several months.

Another type of psychotherapy that has been used to treat ARFID is family-based treatment (FBT). FBT involves the whole family in the treatment process, with the aim of supporting the individual with ARFID to increase their food intake and overcome their fears and anxieties.

In the UK, FBT is often provided by specialist eating disorder teams or child and adolescent mental health services. The treatment typically involves several phases, starting with weight restoration and moving towards the re-introduction of a wider range of foods.

Exposure Therapy

Exposure therapy is another type of therapy that has been used to treat ARFID. Exposure therapy involves gradually exposing individuals to the foods they fear or avoid, with the aim of helping them to become more comfortable with these foods over time.

Exposure therapy can be challenging, and it is important that it is carried out in a safe and supportive environment with the guidance of a trained therapist. In the UK, exposure therapy is often provided as part of a wider treatment plan that may also include psychotherapy and nutritional support.

Medication

Medication is not typically used as a first-line treatment for ARFID, but it can be helpful in some cases. Medications that have been used to treat ARFID include antidepressants and anti-anxiety medications, which can help to reduce anxiety and improve mood.

In the UK, medication for ARFID is typically prescribed by a specialist mental health professional, such as a psychiatrist or a paediatrician. It is important that medication is used alongside other treatments, such as psychotherapy and nutritional support, to ensure the best possible outcomes.

Nutritional Support

Nutritional support is an important aspect of treatment for ARFID, particularly in cases where individuals are malnourished or at risk of malnutrition. Nutritional support can take many forms, including tube feeding, nutritional supplements, and meal planning and support.

In the UK, nutritional support is often provided by a registered dietitian, who can help individuals with ARFID to develop a healthy and balanced eating plan that meets their nutritional needs. In some cases, tube feeding or nutritional supplements may be necessary to ensure adequate nutrition.

In addition to these formal treatment options, there are also several self-help strategies that can be helpful for individuals with ARFID. These may include:

- Keeping a food diary to track food intake and identify patterns and triggers related to eating
- Setting small, achievable goals for increasing food intake and trying new foods
- Practicing relaxation techniques, such as deep breathing or progressive muscle relaxation, to reduce anxiety and stress related to food and eating

Engaging in regular physical activity to improve appetite and overall health
Seeking support from family and friends, or from support groups and online communities for individuals with ARFID
It is important to note that treatment for ARFID is not a one-size-fits-all approach, and what works for one individual may not work for another. It may take time to find the right combination of treatments that work for an individual with ARFID, and it is important to approach treatment with patience and persistence.

In the UK, there are several resources available for individuals with ARFID and their families and caregivers. These may include specialist eating disorder services, child and adolescent mental health services, and community-based support groups.

It is also important to note that there may be barriers to accessing treatment for ARFID, particularly in areas where specialist services are limited or not available. In these cases, it may be helpful to speak to a GP or healthcare professional to explore alternative treatment options, such as online therapy or self-help resources.

Overall, treatment for ARFID in the UK is a collaborative effort that involves healthcare professionals, individuals with ARFID, and their families and caregivers. With the right support and treatment, individuals with ARFID can overcome their fears and anxieties related to food and eating, and develop a healthy and balanced relationship with food.

Chapter 11: Cognitive Behavioral Therapy for ARFID

Cognitive Behavioral Therapy (CBT) is a well-established form of psychological therapy that has been used to treat a range of mental health conditions, including anxiety, depression, and eating disorders. In recent years, CBT has emerged as an effective treatment for Avoidant/Restrictive Food Intake Disorder (ARFID) in both children and adults.

CBT is a goal-oriented therapy that aims to identify and change negative thoughts and behaviors that contribute to mental health problems. In the context of ARFID, CBT can help individuals with ARFID change their thoughts and behaviors related to food and eating, and develop more positive and adaptive coping strategies.

The first step in CBT for ARFID is to conduct a thorough assessment of the individual's symptoms, history, and current situation. This may involve a combination of interviews, questionnaires, and assessments of physical health and nutritional status. Based on this assessment, the therapist will develop a treatment plan tailored to the individual's specific needs and goals.

The treatment plan will typically involve a series of weekly or bi-weekly sessions with the therapist, lasting between 50 and 90 minutes each. During these sessions, the therapist will use a range of CBT techniques to help the individual with ARFID challenge their negative thoughts and behaviors, and develop more adaptive coping strategies.

One of the key techniques used in CBT for ARFID is cognitive restructuring. This involves identifying and challenging negative thoughts and beliefs related to food and eating, and replacing them with more positive and realistic ones. For example, an individual with ARFID may believe that all vegetables are "disgusting" and "unhealthy", and therefore refuse to eat them. Through cognitive restructuring, the therapist can help the individual challenge these negative beliefs and develop more balanced and positive thoughts about vegetables, such as "some vegetables may not be my favorite, but they are important for my health and well-being".

Another important technique used in CBT for ARFID is exposure therapy. This involves gradually and systematically exposing the individual to foods and eating situations that they find challenging, in a safe and supportive environment. For example, the therapist may start by asking the individual to look at pictures of foods they find challenging, and then gradually progress to smelling, touching, and eventually tasting the foods. Through exposure therapy, the individual can learn to tolerate and even enjoy a wider range of foods, and develop more positive associations with eating.

In addition to cognitive restructuring and exposure therapy, CBT for ARFID may also involve other techniques such as behavioral experiments, problem-solving skills training, and relaxation training. The therapist will work closely with the individual to develop a treatment plan that is tailored to their specific needs and goals, and adjust the plan as needed based on their progress and feedback.

CBT for ARFID is typically provided by a qualified and experienced mental health professional, such as a psychologist or psychotherapist. In the UK, CBT for ARFID may be available through the National Health Service (NHS) or through private healthcare providers. The availability of CBT for ARFID may vary depending on the individual's location and the resources available in their area.

In the UK, there are also several national organizations that provide support and information for individuals with ARFID and their families, including Beat, the UK's leading eating disorder charity. Beat offers a range of support services, including a helpline, online support groups, and resources for individuals and families affected by ARFID and other eating disorders. The NHS also provides information and resources on ARFID on its website, including guidance for healthcare professionals on how to diagnose and treat ARFID.

It is important to note that while CBT can be an effective treatment for ARFID, it may not be suitable or effective for everyone. In some cases, additional or alternative treatments may be necessary, such as family-based therapy, occupational therapy, or medical interventions.

It is also important to recognize that ARFID is a complex and multifaceted condition that may require a multidisciplinary approach to treatment. This may involve collaboration between mental health professionals, dietitians, physicians, and other healthcare providers to address the individual's physical, emotional, and nutritional needs.

Overall, CBT is a promising treatment option for individuals with ARFID in the UK. Through cognitive restructuring, exposure therapy, and other techniques, individuals with ARFID can learn to challenge their negative thoughts and behaviors around food, and develop more adaptive coping strategies. By working closely with qualified mental health professionals and other healthcare providers, individuals with ARFID can receive the support and resources they need to overcome this challenging condition and lead a healthy and fulfilling life.

Chapter 12: Family-Based Treatment for ARFID in the UK

Family-based treatment (FBT) is a type of psychotherapy that has shown promise in the treatment of Avoidant/Restrictive Food Intake Disorder (ARFID). This approach involves the family in the treatment process, with the aim of improving the individual's relationship with food and their overall quality of life. In the UK, FBT is a commonly used approach for treating ARFID in children and adolescents, and is typically offered through the National Health Service (NHS).

In FBT, the family is seen as an integral part of the treatment team. Parents are taught how to help their child overcome their fear and anxiety around food, and to gradually introduce new foods into their diet. The treatment typically involves three phases, each with a specific focus and set of goals.

Phase One: Psychoeducation and Weight Restoration

The first phase of FBT is focused on psychoeducation, which involves educating the family about ARFID and the importance of nutritional rehabilitation. This phase is also focused on weight restoration, as many individuals with ARFID are underweight or malnourished. Parents are taught how to monitor their child's food intake, and may be required to prepare meals and snacks for their child.

In the UK, FBT is typically provided through NHS eating disorder services, which offer a multidisciplinary team approach. This may include a consultant psychiatrist, a clinical psychologist, a specialist dietitian, and a family therapist. The team works together to provide comprehensive support to the family, and to tailor the treatment to the specific needs of the individual.

Phase Two: Empowering the Adolescent

The second phase of FBT involves empowering the adolescent to take control of their own eating. This is typically done by gradually increasing their exposure to new foods, and encouraging them to take an active role in meal planning and preparation. Parents are taught how to support their child without taking control of their eating, and how to work collaboratively with their child to overcome any barriers to progress.

In the UK, FBT is typically provided on an outpatient basis, with regular appointments with the multidisciplinary team. The team may also provide support through phone or email contact between appointments.

Phase Three: Consolidation and Relapse Prevention

The third and final phase of FBT is focused on consolidation and relapse prevention. This involves consolidating the gains made in the first two phases, and developing strategies to prevent relapse. Parents are taught how to monitor their child's progress and intervene if there are signs of relapse. The team may also provide ongoing support and monitoring to ensure that the individual maintains their progress over the long term.

While FBT has shown promise in the treatment of ARFID, it is not a one-size-fits-all approach. The success of the treatment depends on a variety of factors, including the severity of the individual's symptoms, their age, and their willingness to participate in the treatment. In some cases, medication may also be used in conjunction with FBT to help manage anxiety or other co-occurring conditions.

In the UK, there is a growing awareness of the importance of early intervention in the treatment of ARFID. The NHS has implemented a variety of initiatives aimed at improving access to treatment for individuals with ARFID, including increased training for healthcare professionals, and the development of specialized ARFID services. However, there is still much work to be done to ensure that all individuals with ARFID have access to the care they need.

One of the challenges of providing FBT in the UK is the limited availability of specialized eating disorder services. This can result in long waiting lists and limited access to care for individuals with ARFID. There is also a need for greater awareness and understanding of ARFID among healthcare professionals and the general public, in order to reduce the stigma associated with the disorder and promote early intervention.

Another challenge is the cost of treatment. While FBT is offered through the NHS in the UK, there may be additional costs associated with private treatment or travel to specialized eating disorder services. This can create barriers to access for individuals and families who may not have the financial resources to afford treatment.

Despite these challenges, there is hope for individuals with ARFID in the UK. With increased awareness and understanding of the disorder, as well as ongoing research into effective treatments, there is the potential for significant progress in the years ahead. It is important for individuals and families affected by ARFID to seek support and to advocate for greater access to care, in order to achieve the best possible outcomes.

In addition to FBT, there are other types of psychotherapy that may be helpful in the treatment of ARFID, such as cognitive-behavioral therapy (CBT) and exposure therapy. These approaches involve gradually exposing the individual to feared foods in a safe and controlled environment, in order to reduce anxiety and increase acceptance of new foods.

It is important to note that ARFID can have significant long-term consequences if left untreated, including malnutrition, growth impairment, and impaired social and emotional development. As such, early intervention is critical in order to promote positive outcomes and prevent further harm.

In conclusion, family-based treatment is a promising approach to the treatment of ARFID in the UK, and is typically offered through the NHS eating disorder services. While there are challenges associated with providing access to care, there is hope for individuals and families affected by ARFID. With increased awareness, understanding, and access to effective treatments, there is the potential for significant progress in the years ahead.

Chapter 13: Exposure Therapy for ARFID

Exposure therapy is a type of behavioural therapy that involves gradually exposing individuals to the feared food or situation in a controlled and safe environment. The goal of exposure therapy for ARFID is to increase the individual's comfort with new foods and decrease their fear and avoidance. In the UK, exposure therapy is often used as part of a comprehensive treatment plan for individuals with ARFID.

When considering exposure therapy as a treatment option for ARFID, it is important to work with a healthcare professional who is experienced in this type of therapy. This may include a clinical psychologist, cognitive behavioural therapist or specialist eating disorder dietitian. These professionals can help create a tailored treatment plan based on the individual's specific needs and goals.

The first step in exposure therapy is to identify the individual's fear hierarchy, which is a list of feared foods or situations ranked in order of difficulty. This hierarchy is used as a guide for gradually exposing the individual to the feared foods or situations, starting with the least feared and progressing to the most feared.

Exposure therapy can take many forms, including:

Sensory exposure: This involves exposing the individual to the look, smell, texture and taste of the feared food in a safe and controlled environment. The individual may start by simply looking at the food or touching it, before progressing to holding it or putting it in their mouth.

Cognitive exposure: This involves challenging the individual's thoughts and beliefs about the feared food or situation. The therapist may ask the individual to write down their negative thoughts and then challenge them with evidence or alternative thoughts.

In vivo exposure: This involves exposing the individual to the feared food or situation in real life, outside of the therapy session. This may involve going to a restaurant or trying a new food at home.

Exposure therapy is often done in a gradual and structured way, with each exposure session building on the previous one. The therapist will work closely with the individual to ensure that they are comfortable and ready to progress to the next step. The therapist may also provide support and guidance to help the individual cope with any anxiety or discomfort that may arise during the exposure sessions.

While exposure therapy can be effective in helping individuals with ARFID increase their comfort with new foods, it is important to note that it may not be suitable for everyone. For example, individuals with severe food aversions or sensory issues may find exposure therapy too challenging. It is important to work closely with a healthcare professional to determine whether exposure therapy is the right treatment option.

In addition to exposure therapy, there are other treatments that may be used to treat ARFID in the UK, including cognitive behavioural therapy (CBT) and family-based treatment (FBT).

CBT is a form of talking therapy that focuses on changing negative thoughts and behaviours. In the context of ARFID, CBT may involve identifying and challenging negative thoughts and beliefs about food, as well as developing practical strategies for trying new foods.

FBT is a type of treatment that involves the whole family in the treatment process. In the context of ARFID, FBT may involve the family working together to gradually introduce new foods and support the individual in trying them.

In addition to these therapies, nutritional support may also be an important part of the treatment plan for individuals with ARFID. This may include working with a registered dietitian to develop a balanced and nutritious meal plan, as well as providing supplements or nutritional support as needed.

In conclusion, exposure therapy is a valuable treatment option for individuals with ARFID in the UK. When done in a safe and controlled environment with the guidance of a healthcare professional, exposure therapy can help individuals increase their comfort with new foods and decrease their fear and avoidance. It is important to work closely with a healthcare professional to determine whether exposure therapy is the right treatment option and to develop a comprehensive treatment plan that may include other therapies and nutritional support.

It is also important to note that the availability of ARFID treatment options in the UK may vary depending on where an individual lives and their access to healthcare services. Some regions may have more specialised eating disorder services than others, and waiting times for treatment may also vary.

However, there are a number of organisations and resources available in the UK to support individuals with ARFID and their families. These may include local eating disorder charities, support groups, and online resources such as the Beat Eating Disorders website.

It is also important to recognise that recovery from ARFID can be a long and challenging process. It may involve setbacks and relapses, but with the right support and treatment, individuals with ARFID can make progress towards a more varied and balanced diet.

Overall, exposure therapy is a promising treatment option for individuals with ARFID in the UK, and it is important to work closely with healthcare professionals to develop a personalised treatment plan that addresses the individual's specific needs and goals. With the right support, individuals with ARFID can overcome their fear and avoidance of new foods and improve their overall quality of life.

Chapter 14: Medication for ARFID

In the United Kingdom, medication is sometimes used as part of the treatment plan for Avoidant/Restrictive Food Intake Disorder (ARFID). However, it is important to note that medication should not be seen as a standalone treatment for ARFID, and should always be used in combination with other forms of therapy and support.

There are a few different medications that may be prescribed for individuals with ARFID, depending on their specific symptoms and needs. These medications are typically prescribed by a psychiatrist or other mental health professional, and should always be taken under close medical supervision.

One medication that may be prescribed for ARFID is an antidepressant. Antidepressants can be helpful for individuals with ARFID who also have symptoms of depression or anxiety. These medications work by altering the levels of certain chemicals in the brain, known as neurotransmitters, which can improve mood and reduce feelings of anxiety. It is important to note that antidepressants can take several weeks to start working, and may have some side effects, so it is important to discuss these potential risks and benefits with a healthcare provider.

Another medication that may be prescribed for ARFID is an antipsychotic. Antipsychotics are typically used to treat symptoms of psychosis, such as hallucinations or delusions. However, they can also be helpful for individuals with ARFID who experience severe anxiety or have a significant aversion to certain foods. These medications can help to reduce feelings of anxiety and increase appetite, which can make it easier for individuals with ARFID to try new foods. Like antidepressants, antipsychotics can have side effects and should be taken under close medical supervision.

Some individuals with ARFID may also benefit from medication to treat co-occurring conditions, such as ADHD or OCD. For example, a medication like Ritalin or Adderall may be prescribed to help improve focus and reduce distractibility in individuals with ARFID and ADHD. Similarly, medication like fluoxetine or sertraline may be prescribed to help reduce symptoms of OCD in individuals with ARFID and OCD.

It is important to note that medication should always be used in combination with other forms of therapy and support for ARFID. Medication can be a helpful tool to reduce symptoms and make it easier to engage in therapy and other forms of treatment, but it is not a standalone solution for ARFID. In addition to medication, individuals with ARFID may benefit from therapy such as cognitive behavioural therapy (CBT) or family-based treatment (FBT), as well as support from a registered dietitian.

It is also important to note that medication is not always the right choice for every individual with ARFID. There are potential risks and side effects associated with medication, and it is important to carefully weigh the potential benefits and risks before starting any medication. It is also important to work closely with a mental health professional to monitor any side effects or changes in symptoms.

In the UK, access to medication for ARFID may depend on a number of factors, including the individual's age, the severity of their symptoms, and their access to mental health services. For children and young people with ARFID, medication may be prescribed by a specialist child and adolescent mental health service (CAMHS). For adults with ARFID, medication may be prescribed by a psychiatrist or other mental health professional.

In some cases, access to medication for ARFID may be limited due to funding constraints or a lack of available services in certain areas. This highlights the need for increased awareness and understanding of ARFID in the UK, as well as increased investment in mental health services to ensure that individuals with ARFID have access to the support and resources they need to recover.

It is also important to note that medication is just one aspect of a comprehensive treatment plan for ARFID. Along with therapy and support, individuals with ARFID may also benefit from nutritional counselling, occupational therapy, and other forms of support. Family-based treatment, in particular, has been shown to be effective for children and adolescents with ARFID, and involves working closely with parents and caregivers to help children overcome their aversions to certain foods and increase their food intake.

In the UK, there are a number of organizations and resources available for individuals with ARFID and their families, including Beat, the UK's leading eating disorder charity, and the National Centre for Eating Disorders (NCFED). These organizations offer support groups, information, and resources for individuals with ARFID and their families, and can be a valuable source of support for those struggling with the disorder.

In conclusion, medication can be a useful tool in the treatment of ARFID in the UK, particularly for individuals who experience co-occurring conditions such as depression, anxiety, or OCD. However, it is important to remember that medication should not be seen as a standalone treatment for ARFID, and should always be used in combination with other forms of therapy and support. Individuals with ARFID and their families should work closely with mental health professionals and other healthcare providers to develop a comprehensive treatment plan that addresses all aspects of the disorder and promotes long-term recovery.

Chapter 15: Nutritional Support for ARFID

In the UK, individuals with ARFID may receive nutritional support as part of their treatment plan. Nutritional support can be provided in a variety of ways, including tube feeding, oral nutritional supplements, and modified diets. The goal of nutritional support is to ensure that individuals with ARFID are meeting their nutritional needs and maintaining their health while they work on improving their relationship with food.

Tube Feeding

Tube feeding, also known as enteral feeding, involves the delivery of nutrients directly into the digestive tract through a tube. This may be necessary for individuals with ARFID who are unable to consume enough food orally to meet their nutritional needs. Tube feeding can be temporary or long-term, depending on the individual's needs.

There are several different types of tubes that can be used for feeding, including nasogastric tubes, gastrostomy tubes, and jejunostomy tubes. Nasogastric tubes are inserted through the nose and down into the stomach, while gastrostomy and jejunostomy tubes are surgically inserted through the skin and into the stomach or small intestine. The type of tube used will depend on the individual's specific needs and medical history.

Oral Nutritional Supplements

Oral nutritional supplements (ONS) are liquid or semi-solid products that are designed to provide a complete source of nutrition. ONS can be used as a supplement to a regular diet or as a sole source of nutrition for individuals who are unable to consume food orally.

ONS come in a variety of flavours and textures to suit individual preferences, and can be prescribed by a doctor or registered dietitian. They are typically available in the form of a drink or a pudding-like consistency. ONS can be purchased over the counter or prescribed by a healthcare professional.

Modified Diets

Modified diets involve altering the texture, consistency, or nutrient content of food to make it easier for individuals with ARFID to consume. This may include blending food to create a smooth consistency, or fortifying foods with additional nutrients.

Modified diets can be prescribed by a registered dietitian, who will work with the individual to create a plan that meets their specific nutritional needs. This may involve adding in additional sources of protein, carbohydrates, and other nutrients to ensure that the individual is getting a balanced diet.

Challenges of Nutritional Support for ARFID

While nutritional support can be a helpful tool in the treatment of ARFID, there are also challenges that must be addressed. For example, individuals with ARFID may have strong aversions to certain textures or flavours, which can make it difficult to find an ONS or modified diet that they are willing to consume.

In addition, tube feeding and modified diets can be expensive, and may not be covered by insurance or the NHS. This can create financial barriers to accessing these forms of nutritional support, which can be a major challenge for individuals and families.

Finally, nutritional support should not be seen as a long-term solution for ARFID. While it can be helpful in the short-term to ensure that individuals are meeting their nutritional needs, the ultimate goal of treatment should be to help individuals develop a healthier relationship with food and overcome their aversions to certain foods.

Conclusion

Nutritional support can be a helpful tool in the treatment of ARFID in the UK. Tube feeding, oral nutritional supplements, and modified diets can all be used to ensure that individuals with ARFID are meeting their nutritional needs and maintaining their health while they work on improving their relationship with food. However, there are also challenges associated with these forms of support, and it is important to work with a healthcare professional to determine the best course of treatment for each individual. Ultimately, the goal of treatment should be to help individuals with ARFID develop a healthier relationship with food, so that they can enjoy a wide variety of foods and feel confident in their ability to meet their nutritional needs.

In addition to nutritional support, individuals with ARFID may benefit from other forms of treatment, such as cognitive-behavioural therapy (CBT) and exposure therapy. CBT can help individuals identify and challenge their negative thoughts and beliefs about food, while exposure therapy can help them gradually desensitize to the foods they fear or avoid.

Overall, the treatment of ARFID in the UK requires a multidisciplinary approach, involving healthcare professionals from a variety of disciplines, including dietitians, therapists, and physicians. This approach can help to ensure that individuals with ARFID receive comprehensive, individualized care that addresses all aspects of their condition.

It is also important to note that ARFID can have a significant impact on an individual's mental health and quality of life. Individuals with ARFID may experience anxiety, depression, social isolation, and other mental health issues as a result of their condition. Therefore, it is important to address both the physical and psychological aspects of ARFID in order to promote overall health and well-being.

In conclusion, nutritional support can be an important part of the treatment of ARFID in the UK. Tube feeding, oral nutritional supplements, and modified diets can all be used to ensure that individuals with ARFID are meeting their nutritional needs while they work on improving their relationship with food. However, it is important to address the challenges associated with these forms of support, and to take a multidisciplinary approach to treatment that addresses both the physical and psychological aspects of ARFID. With the right care and support, individuals with ARFID can learn to enjoy a wide variety of foods and lead happy, healthy lives.

Chapter 16: Support for Families and Caregivers

Families and caregivers of individuals with Avoidant/Restrictive Food Intake Disorder (ARFID) can face numerous challenges in supporting their loved ones. In the UK, ARFID is a relatively new diagnosis and there is still limited awareness and understanding of the condition amongst the general public, healthcare professionals and even educators. This can result in families and caregivers feeling isolated and unsupported. In this chapter, we will explore the different types of support available for families and caregivers of individuals with ARFID in the UK.

Support from healthcare professionals

In the UK, healthcare professionals such as GPs, paediatricians, dietitians and mental health practitioners are the main point of contact for families and caregivers seeking support for ARFID. These professionals play a critical role in the diagnosis, treatment and ongoing management of ARFID. Families and caregivers are encouraged to seek help as soon as possible if they suspect that their loved one has ARFID. Early intervention and support can improve the long-term outcomes for individuals with ARFID.

The National Institute for Health and Care Excellence (NICE) provides guidelines for the treatment of eating disorders in the UK. These guidelines recommend a multidisciplinary approach involving medical, psychological and nutritional support. Families and caregivers should work with their healthcare team to develop a tailored treatment plan for their loved one. This may involve Cognitive Behavioural Therapy (CBT), Family-Based Treatment (FBT), medication or nutritional support.

Support from charities and support groups

There are several charities and support groups in the UK that provide information, advice and support to families and caregivers of individuals with ARFID. These include:

Beat Eating Disorders: Beat is the UK's leading eating disorder charity. They provide helplines, online support groups, peer support and practical advice for families and caregivers of individuals with eating disorders.

The National Centre for Eating Disorders (NCFED): NCFED provides training, workshops and online resources for families and caregivers of individuals with eating disorders. They also offer support for individuals with ARFID.

First Steps ED: First Steps is a charity that provides support, counselling and therapy for individuals with eating disorders and their families. They have a specialist ARFID service for children and young people.

Support from education providers

Children and young people with ARFID may struggle to eat at school or college due to anxiety, sensory issues or other reasons. Families and caregivers should work with their education providers to develop a plan that supports their loved one's needs. This may involve working with a school nurse or school meals service to provide suitable food options, allowing the child to eat in a quiet space or providing extra support during meal times.

The UK government has developed guidelines for school meals and food standards in schools. These guidelines aim to ensure that children and young people have access to healthy and nutritious food options. Families and caregivers of children with ARFID can work with their education providers to ensure that these guidelines are being met.

Support for families and caregivers can be critical in helping individuals with ARFID to recover and manage their condition. Families and caregivers should not be afraid to seek help and support, and should work closely with healthcare professionals, charities and education providers to develop a tailored support plan for their loved one.

It is also worth noting that while the current provision of ARFID care in the UK is limited, there is growing awareness and momentum towards better understanding, recognition and investment in ARFID in the UK, with a growing number of specialist eating disorder centres, such as the Royal London Hospital and North London Priory, starting to offer ARFID-specific services. Families and caregivers can also play an important role in advocating for better support and resources for ARFID in the UK, by sharing their experiences with healthcare professionals, charities and education providers, and raising awareness of ARFID in their local communities.

In addition, families and caregivers should also prioritise self-care and support for themselves, as caring for a loved one with ARFID can be challenging and stressful. This may involve seeking their own therapy, attending support groups or seeking respite care. The UK government also provides a range of benefits and support for carers, including financial assistance and access to respite care.

It is important to note that ARFID can be a complex and challenging condition to manage, and there may be times when families and caregivers may need additional support or intervention. This may include hospitalisation or access to specialist ARFID treatment centres. Families and caregivers should work closely with their healthcare professionals to develop a plan that meets their loved one's needs and ensures their safety and wellbeing.

In conclusion, families and caregivers of individuals with ARFID in the UK have access to a range of support services, including healthcare professionals, charities and education providers. Families and caregivers should not hesitate to seek help and support, and should work closely with these services to develop a tailored support plan for their loved one. It is also important for families and caregivers to prioritise self-care and support for themselves, and to advocate for better support and resources for ARFID in the UK. With early intervention and ongoing support, individuals with ARFID can recover and manage their condition, and families and caregivers can play a critical role in this process.

Chapter 17: Coping Strategies for ARFID

Individuals with Avoidant/Restrictive Food Intake Disorder (ARFID) face significant challenges related to food and eating, which can lead to social isolation and poor physical health outcomes. Coping strategies can help individuals with ARFID manage their symptoms and improve their quality of life. In this chapter, we will discuss practical tips and coping strategies for individuals with ARFID in the UK.

Meal Planning and Preparation

Meal planning and preparation can help individuals with ARFID feel more in control of their food intake and reduce anxiety related to meal times. A registered dietitian can help develop a meal plan that accommodates an individual's food preferences and restrictions. Meal planning can also help individuals with ARFID anticipate and prepare for meals outside the home, such as at work or social events.

Individuals with ARFID may benefit from involving themselves in meal preparation, such as grocery shopping or cooking. This can increase exposure to new foods and increase their comfort level with trying new foods. It is important to remember that it is okay to start small and take baby steps when trying new foods. Trying a new recipe or cooking method can be a way to introduce new foods in a safe and controlled environment.

Food Exposure Exercises

Exposure therapy is a common form of treatment for individuals with ARFID. Exposure exercises involve gradually exposing individuals to new foods or foods that are challenging for them. In the UK, a registered dietitian or therapist can guide individuals through exposure exercises in a controlled and supportive environment.

Individuals with ARFID can also practice exposure exercises on their own. This can involve gradually increasing the amount or variety of a food over time. For example, an individual may start by smelling a new food or looking at a picture of it, then progress to touching it or taking a small bite. It is important to remember that exposure exercises should be done at a pace that is comfortable for the individual and should not cause significant distress or anxiety.

Self-Care

Self-care can be an important part of coping with ARFID. It is important to prioritize self-care activities that promote mental and physical health. This can include exercise, relaxation techniques, and getting enough sleep.

Stress can exacerbate symptoms of ARFID, so it is important to find healthy ways to manage stress. This can include meditation, deep breathing exercises, or talking to a therapist. Engaging in hobbies or activities that bring joy and relaxation can also help reduce stress and promote mental health.

Social Situations

Social situations involving food can be challenging for individuals with ARFID. It can be helpful to plan ahead for social events, such as bringing safe foods or eating before the event. It can also be helpful to have a support person, such as a friend or family member, who understands and supports the individual's dietary restrictions and can provide encouragement and reassurance during social events.

It is important to communicate with others about dietary restrictions and preferences, but it is also important to avoid excessive explanation or apology. A simple statement of "I have dietary restrictions" or "I'm not a big fan of that food" can be sufficient without going into too much detail.

Conclusion

Coping with ARFID can be challenging, but practical tips and coping strategies can help individuals with ARFID manage their symptoms and improve their quality of life. Meal planning and preparation, food exposure exercises, self-care, and managing social situations can all be part of an individualized coping plan for ARFID. It is important to remember that treatment for ARFID can be effective, and seeking help from a registered dietitian or mental health professional is a crucial step in managing symptoms and improving quality of life.

Chapter 18: Advocacy and Awareness for ARFID

ARFID is a relatively new diagnosis and is not yet widely recognized or understood in the UK. This lack of awareness can make it challenging for individuals with ARFID to receive appropriate treatment and support. Advocacy and awareness efforts are essential to ensure that individuals with ARFID can access the care they need.

There are several advocacy and awareness efforts underway in the UK to improve understanding and support for ARFID. The first step towards increasing awareness is to educate healthcare professionals on the condition. In 2020, the UK's National Institute for Health and Care Excellence (NICE) released guidelines on the identification, assessment, and treatment of ARFID. These guidelines are designed to help healthcare professionals recognize the signs and symptoms of ARFID and provide appropriate treatment and support.

In addition to NICE guidelines, there are several organizations and charities in the UK dedicated to raising awareness and providing support for individuals with ARFID and their families. One such organization is ARFID UK, a non-profit organization that provides information, resources, and support to individuals with ARFID and their families. ARFID UK works to raise awareness of the condition through social media campaigns, educational resources, and fundraising events.

Another organization that advocates for individuals with ARFID is Beat, the UK's leading eating disorder charity. Beat provides support and information for individuals with all types of eating disorders, including ARFID. The charity has developed an ARFID-specific page on its website, providing information on the condition, symptoms, and treatment options. Beat also runs a helpline for individuals with eating disorders and their families, providing support and advice on a range of issues related to ARFID and other eating disorders.

While these organizations are doing important work, more needs to be done to increase awareness and understanding of ARFID in the UK. One area where advocacy efforts could be focused is on improving the availability of treatment and support services for individuals with ARFID. Currently, there are few specialized treatment centers in the UK that offer specific programs for individuals with ARFID. This can make it challenging for individuals with ARFID to access appropriate care and support.

One way to address this issue is to increase funding for research into ARFID and its treatment. This could help identify new approaches to treating the condition and improve the availability of specialized treatment centers in the UK. Another approach would be to increase training and education for healthcare professionals on the diagnosis and treatment of ARFID. This could help ensure that individuals with ARFID receive appropriate care and support from the outset.

Another area where advocacy efforts could be focused is on reducing the stigma associated with ARFID. Many individuals with ARFID report feeling ashamed or embarrassed about their condition, which can make it challenging to seek help. Increasing awareness and understanding of ARFID in the wider community could help reduce stigma and encourage individuals with ARFID to seek the support they need.

In addition to advocacy efforts, there are steps that individuals with ARFID and their families can take to improve awareness and support. One approach is to share their stories and experiences with ARFID on social media or through personal blogs or vlogs. This can help raise awareness of the condition and provide support for others who may be struggling with similar issues.

Another approach is to work with healthcare professionals to develop a treatment plan that meets their specific needs. This may involve seeking out a specialist treatment center or working with a registered dietitian to develop a meal plan that accommodates their specific food preferences and sensitivities.

In conclusion, advocacy and awareness efforts are essential to ensure that individuals with ARFID can access appropriate treatment and support. While there are several organizations and charities in the UK dedicated to raising awareness and providing support for individuals with ARFID and their families, more needs to be done to improve understanding and access to specialized treatment centers. Increasing funding for research and training for healthcare professionals on the diagnosis and treatment of ARFID could help improve the availability of specialized treatment centers in the UK. Reducing the stigma associated with ARFID is also essential to encourage individuals with ARFID to seek the support they need.

It is important to note that advocacy and awareness efforts for ARFID must be tailored to the unique cultural and societal context of the UK. For example, in some cultures, picky eating or food aversions may be viewed as a sign of defiance or disrespect towards food and culture. It is important to acknowledge these cultural differences and work towards developing a more inclusive understanding and approach to ARFID.

Overall, advocacy and awareness efforts are crucial to improving understanding and support for individuals with ARFID in the UK. Through collaboration between healthcare professionals, organizations, and individuals with ARFID and their families, we can work towards improving access to appropriate treatment and support and reducing the stigma associated with the condition.

Chapter 19: Future Directions for ARFID Research and Treatment

ARFID has gained increasing recognition in recent years, but there is still much to be learned about this condition. In the UK, there has been limited research into ARFID specifically, and much of the research on feeding and eating disorders has focused on anorexia nervosa and bulimia nervosa. However, there are some promising developments in the field of ARFID research and treatment.

One area of research that is gaining traction in the UK is the exploration of the underlying causes of ARFID. While the exact causes of ARFID are not yet fully understood, researchers are beginning to identify potential factors that may contribute to the development of the condition. For example, a recent study conducted by researchers at the University of Glasgow found that children with ARFID were more likely to have experienced gastrointestinal symptoms, such as stomach pain and nausea, in early childhood than children without ARFID. This suggests that there may be a link between gastrointestinal issues and the development of ARFID.

Another area of research that is gaining momentum is the investigation of different treatment approaches for ARFID. While there is currently no standard treatment protocol for ARFID, several promising interventions have been developed, such as cognitive behavioural therapy (CBT), exposure therapy, and family-based treatment (FBT). A recent study conducted by researchers at the University of Oxford found that FBT was effective in treating ARFID in adolescents. The study found that adolescents who received FBT had significant improvements in weight and eating behaviour compared to those who received standard care.

In addition to research on the causes and treatments of ARFID, there is also a growing interest in improving the awareness and understanding of ARFID among healthcare professionals and the general public in the UK. Many individuals with ARFID report feeling misunderstood and stigmatized, and there is a need for greater education and awareness about the condition.

One promising development in this area is the establishment of the UK Eating Disorders Research Network (EDRN), which brings together researchers, clinicians, and patients to advance research on eating disorders, including ARFID. The EDRN has launched several initiatives to improve awareness and understanding of ARFID, such as an online training course for healthcare professionals on the diagnosis and treatment of ARFID.

Another important step towards improving awareness and understanding of ARFID in the UK is the inclusion of ARFID in the latest edition of the International Classification of Diseases (ICD-11), which is used by healthcare professionals to diagnose and classify medical conditions. The inclusion of ARFID in the ICD-11 will help to increase recognition of the condition among healthcare professionals in the UK and around the world.

While there is still much work to be done in the field of ARFID research and treatment in the UK, these developments provide hope for individuals with ARFID and their families. With increased awareness, research, and collaboration, we can continue to improve our understanding of this complex condition and develop more effective treatments to help individuals with ARFID live healthy, fulfilling lives. One important direction for future research in the UK is the exploration of the long-term outcomes of ARFID. While some studies have found that individuals with ARFID may have better physical health outcomes than those with other eating disorders, such as anorexia nervosa, there is limited research on the long-term psychological and social outcomes of ARFID. Understanding these outcomes is essential for developing effective interventions that address the full range of challenges faced by individuals with ARFID.

Another important direction for future research is the investigation of the role of genetics in the development of ARFID. While research on the genetics of eating disorders has focused primarily on anorexia nervosa and bulimia nervosa, there is increasing evidence that genetic factors may play a role in the development of ARFID as well. Identifying specific genetic markers associated with ARFID could help to inform the development of more targeted and effective treatments.

In addition to research, there is also a need for greater resources and support for individuals with ARFID and their families in the UK. Currently, there are limited specialised treatment programmes for ARFID, and many individuals with ARFID struggle to find appropriate care. Improving access to evidence-based treatments and increasing funding for ARFID research could help to address these gaps and improve outcomes for individuals with ARFID.

Another important step towards improving resources and support for individuals with ARFID in the UK is the development of peer support networks and online communities. These networks can provide a valuable source of information, encouragement, and support for individuals with ARFID and their families, who may feel isolated and misunderstood.

In conclusion, while there is still much to be learned about ARFID, there are many promising developments in the field of ARFID research and treatment in the UK. As we continue to improve our understanding of this condition, we can develop more effective interventions and support systems to help individuals with ARFID lead healthy, fulfilling lives.

Chapter 20: Conclusion

In the United Kingdom, awareness of ARFID is still limited among the general population and even some healthcare professionals. However, there are efforts underway to improve understanding and support for individuals with ARFID and their families.

One key initiative is the ARFID UK Network, a group of healthcare professionals, researchers, and individuals with lived experience of ARFID who aim to raise awareness, promote early diagnosis, and improve access to evidence-based treatments. The Network provides resources and support for individuals with ARFID and their families, as well as training opportunities for healthcare professionals.

In addition, the National Institute for Health and Care Excellence (NICE) has recently published guidelines on the assessment and management of eating disorders, including ARFID. The guidelines recommend that healthcare professionals should consider ARFID as a possible diagnosis in individuals with restrictive eating habits, and provide appropriate assessment and treatment.

While progress is being made, there is still much work to be done in terms of improving access to evidence-based treatments for ARFID in the UK. Currently, there is a lack of specialised services for ARFID, and many individuals struggle to access appropriate treatment. This is particularly challenging for individuals living in rural areas, where access to specialist services may be limited.

However, there are steps that can be taken to improve access to treatment. For example, primary care physicians can play an important role in identifying and referring individuals with ARFID to specialist services. In addition, online support groups and resources can provide valuable information and support for individuals and families affected by ARFID.

It is important to recognise that ARFID can have a significant impact on an individual's physical and mental health, as well as their quality of life. However, with early diagnosis and appropriate treatment, recovery is possible. It is important for individuals with ARFID and their families to seek help as soon as possible, and to know that they are not alone.

In conclusion, ARFID is a relatively new diagnosis that is still not widely recognised or understood in the UK. However, there are positive developments in terms of awareness, diagnosis, and treatment, and there are resources and support available for individuals and families affected by ARFID. It is important for healthcare professionals, policymakers, and the general public to continue to learn about ARFID and to work towards improving access to evidence-based treatments for those affected.

10 Hidden Vegetable Recipes

Hidden Veggie Spaghetti Sauce

Ingredients:

1 can (28 oz) crushed tomatoes
1/2 cup finely grated zucchini
1/2 cup finely grated carrots
1/2 cup finely chopped onion
2 cloves garlic, minced
1 teaspoon dried basil
1 teaspoon dried oregano
Salt and pepper to taste
Instructions:

In a large saucepan, sauté the onions and garlic until softened.

Add the grated zucchini and carrots and sauté until tender.

Add the crushed tomatoes and spices, and let simmer for 15-20 minutes.

Serve over your favorite pasta.

Hidden Veggie Meatloaf

Ingredients:

1 lb ground beef
1 cup grated zucchini
1 cup grated carrots
1/2 cup finely chopped onion
1/2 cup breadcrumbs
1/4 cup ketchup
1 egg
Salt and pepper to taste
Instructions:

Preheat oven to 350°F.

Mix all ingredients together in a large bowl.

Grease a loaf pan and pack the mixture in tightly.

Bake for 1 hour, or until fully cooked.

Let cool for a few minutes before slicing and serving.

Hidden Veggie Pizza Sauce

Ingredients:

1 can (28 oz) crushed tomatoes
1/2 cup finely grated zucchini
1/2 cup finely grated carrots
1/2 cup finely chopped onion
2 cloves garlic, minced
1 teaspoon dried basil
1 teaspoon dried oregano
Salt and pepper to taste
Instructions:

In a large saucepan, sauté the onions and garlic until softened.

Add the grated zucchini and carrots and sauté until tender.

Add the crushed tomatoes and spices, and let simmer for 15-20 minutes.

Use as a pizza sauce on your favorite crust, topped with cheese and your favorite toppings.

Hidden Veggie Quesadillas

Ingredients:

1 large bell pepper, chopped
1 small zucchini, chopped
1 small onion, chopped
2 cloves garlic, minced
1 cup cooked black beans
2 cups shredded cheese
4 large flour tortillas
Salt and pepper to taste
Olive oil for cooking
Instructions:

In a large skillet, sauté the bell pepper, zucchini, onion, and garlic until softened.

Add the black beans and cook for an additional 2-3 minutes.

Lay out a tortilla and sprinkle with cheese.

Add a scoop of the veggie mixture on top of the cheese, then top with another sprinkle of cheese.

Fold the tortilla in half and press down lightly.

Heat a small amount of olive oil in a separate skillet and cook the quesadilla until golden brown on both sides.

Repeat with remaining tortillas and veggie mixture.

Hidden Veggie Chicken Nuggets

Ingredients:

1 lb ground chicken
1/2 cup finely grated zucchini
1/2 cup finely grated carrots
1/2 cup breadcrumbs
1 egg
Salt and pepper to taste
Olive oil for cooking
Instructions:

Preheat oven to 375°F.
Mix all ingredients together in a large bowl.
Form the mixture into small nugget shapes.
Heat a small amount of olive oil in a large skillet over medium
heat.

Add the nuggets to the skillet and cook until golden brown on
both sides.

Transfer the nuggets to a baking sheet and bake in the oven
for an additional 10-15 minutes, or until fully cooked.

Serve with your favorite dipping sauce.

Hidden Veggie Meatballs

Ingredients:

1 lb ground beef
1/2 cup finely grated zucchini
1/2 cup finely grated carrots
1/2 cup breadcrumbs
1 egg
Salt and pepper to taste
Olive oil for cooking
Instructions:

Preheat oven to 375°F.

Mix all ingredients together in a large bowl.

Form the mixture into small meatball shapes.

Heat a small amount of olive oil in a large skillet over medium heat.

Add the meatballs to the skillet and cook until browned on all sides.

Transfer the meatballs to a baking sheet and bake in the oven for an additional 10-15 minutes, or until fully cooked.

Serve with your favorite sauce or over spaghetti.

Hidden Veggie Mac and Cheese

Ingredients:

2 cups elbow macaroni
1/2 cup finely grated zucchini
1/2 cup finely grated carrots
1/2 cup finely chopped cauliflower
2 tablespoons butter
2 tablespoons flour
2 cups milk
2 cups shredded cheddar cheese
Salt and pepper to taste
Instructions:

Cook the macaroni according to package directions, adding the zucchini, carrots, and cauliflower during the last 5 minutes of cooking.

While the pasta cooks, melt the butter in a large saucepan over medium heat.

Whisk in the flour and cook for 1-2 minutes, or until lightly browned.

Slowly add the milk, whisking constantly to prevent lumps.

Cook the mixture, whisking frequently, until it thickens and begins to bubble.

Stir in the cheese until melted and smooth.

Drain the pasta and veggies and add them to the cheese sauce.

Stir to combine and serve hot.

Hidden Veggie Tater Tots

Ingredients:

2 cups grated potatoes
1/2 cup finely grated zucchini
1/2 cup finely grated carrots
1/4 cup flour
1 egg
Salt and pepper to taste
Oil for frying
Instructions:

Mix all ingredients together in a large bowl.

Heat a small amount of oil in a large skillet over medium-high heat.

Drop spoonfuls of the mixture into the hot oil and flatten slightly with a spatula.

Cook until golden brown on both sides.

Serve hot with ketchup or your favorite dipping sauce.

Hidden Veggie Smoothie

Ingredients:

1 cup fresh spinach
1/2 cup frozen berries
1/2 cup chopped cucumber
1/2 cup chopped carrots
1/2 cup plain Greek yogurt
1/2 cup unsweetened almond milk
1 tablespoon honey
Instructions:

Combine all ingredients in a blender and blend until smooth.

Add more almond milk if needed to reach desired consistency.

Serve immediately.

Hidden Veggie Muffins

Ingredients:

1 cup finely grated zucchini
1/2 cup finely grated carrots
2 cups all-purpose flour
1/2 cup sugar
1 teaspoon baking powder

1/2 teaspoon baking soda
1/2 teaspoon salt
1/2 cup unsweetened applesauce
1/2 cup milk
1 egg
1 teaspoon vanilla extract
Instructions:

Preheat oven to 375°F and grease a muffin tin.
In a large bowl, mix together the zucchini, carrots, flour,
sugar, baking powder, baking soda, and salt.
In a separate bowl, whisk together the applesauce, milk, egg,
and vanilla extract.
Add the wet ingredients to the dry ingredients and mix until
just combined.
Spoon the batter into the prepared muffin tin, filling each
muffin cup about 2/3 full.
Bake for 20-25 minutes, or until a toothpick inserted in the
center of a muffin comes out clean.
Cool in the pan for 5 minutes before transferring to a wire rack
to cool completely.

These 10 hidden vegetable recipes are a great way to sneak in some extra nutrition into your meals and snacks without sacrificing flavor. Try them out and see how your family responds!

Thank you for taking the time to read this Introduction to a Neurodiverse World book.
We have a range of books within this series that are steadily being released.
Topics Cover

- Autism
- ADHD
- Sensory Processing Disorder (SPD)
- Pathological Demand Avoidance (PDA)
- Avoidant Restrictive Food Intake Disorder (ARFID)

We also post weekly Articles on our website and our social media sites (links Below)

Divergent Consultants Ltd are accredited Counsellors and Psychotherapists who specialize in Spectrum Disorders.

Started by Gareth Croot when his 3-year-old Non-Verbal son was diagnosed with Autism Spectrum Disorder, Global Development Delay and Hypermobility.
This lead his family on a journey resulting in his 12 year old daughter starting the ASD diagnostic pathway and Gareth also being diagnosed with Autism, PDA, Hypermobility and currently awaiting ADHD assessment.
Divergent Consultants offer introduction to Autism Courses, Sleep Therapy Courses, Pre and Post diagnosis counselling for parents and newly diagnosed adults as well as general support functions.
you can visit us at www.divergentconsultants.co.uk
Facebook https://www.facebook.com/people/Divergent-Consultants/100088643106730/
TikTok https://www.tiktok.com/divergentconsultants
Instagram
https://www.instagram.com/divergent_consultants/

www.ingramcontent.com/pod-product-compliance
Lightning Source LLC
Chambersburg PA
CBHW051834250726
48659CB00005B/1826